Collins

Livemocha **ACTIVE ITALIAN**

DA318248

HarperCollins Publishers
77–85 Fulham Palace Road
London W6 8JB
Great Britain

www.collinslanguage.com

First edition 2011

Reprint 10 9 8 7 6 5 4 3 2 1 0
© HarperCollins Publishers 2011

ISBN (UK edition) 978-0-00-737353-6
ISBN (export edition) 978-0-00-741980-7
ISBN (US edition) 978-0-87779-557-5

Collins® is a registered trademark of HarperCollins Publishers Limited

A catalogue record for this book is available from the British Library

Typeset by Macmillan Publishing Services

Audio material recorded and produced by Networks SRL, Milan

Printed and Bound in China by Leo Paper Products Ltd.
Series Editor: Rob Scriven

INTRODUCTION

Welcome to your Livemocha Active Italian experience! This new course goes above and beyond what a traditional book-based course can offer. With its focus on online learning, Active Italian provides the opportunity not just to study but to experience the language for yourself by interacting with native speakers online.

Why go online?

Studying a language online allows you to learn in a more natural atmosphere – watching people interact in a **video** is far more lifelike than listening to conversations on a CD. After watching a video dialog, you will be walked through an explanation of some of the **grammar** and **vocabulary** items that were introduced in the new dialog. Then, by completing a variety of **interactive quizzes**, the system will instantly be able to tell you how well you are doing. You can then **talk online** with native Italian speakers to practice what you've learned.

Who else is online?

Livemocha boasts over 7 million members and is growing every day. These members are online for the same reason as you – to learn and experience a new language. Native Italian-speaking members will be happy to read through your written and spoken submissions and to give you feedback on how you're doing. You can also connect with people who want to chat in any given language – interaction on an informal, nonacademic basis is an ideal way for you to perfect your language skills.

What do the books do?

The four accompanying books are designed to complement the online course – the dialogs for all of the videos that you can watch online are available here for you to study whenever you don't have access to the Internet. You will also find all of the Grammar and Vocabulary sections explained in the books, plus the culture notes to teach you a little about Italy.

LEVEL 2

This book is the second of four. It corresponds with Level 2 of the online course.

Level 2 is ideal for students who can understand a simple conversation but who may still have difficulty taking part.

What you will learn

- How to buy tickets, ask for information, and understand directions
- How to make plans, understand suggestions and accept invitations
- How to form and use commands, talk about possession, and make comparisons
- How to form the perfect tense using *avere*
- Vocabulary for sports, museums, more jobs, city and town, clothes, colors, months and daily routines

 Every time you see this coffee cup symbol in these books, it indicates the presence of a pathway – a guide to exactly where you can find that particular piece of content online. Log on at www.livemocha.com and follow the path to find the online version of what you are studying in the book.

Video Dialog

As they finish their drinks, Michele and the waiter give Giulia directions to some local stores.

 Active Italian: Level 1 > Unit 3 > Lesson 1 > Video dialog

1

Lesson 1: Planning a trip to the museum

- » How to ask for help: *Mi può aiutare?*
- » How to say you are going to a place: *andare a* (or *al, alla, all'*, etc.)...
- » How to modify adjectives using adverbs: *abbastanza, molto, troppo*, etc.
- » The difference between *Bisogna...* and *Sarebbe meglio....*
- » How to say that something happens regularly on a particular day: *il lunedì, il sabato*, etc.
- » How to make nouns and adjectives agree.

Lesson 2: Getting directions to a museum

- » Possessive adjectives "my," "your," "his," "our," etc.: *mio, tuo, suo, nostro*, etc.
- » How to say "my favorite...": *il mio... preferito.*
- » Different ways of saying "Not at all."
- » How to give directions: *Giri a sinistra/destra.*
- » The word *su* (on) and how it combines with the direct articles to become *sul, sullu, sull'*, etc.

UNIT 1 › LESSON 1

Planning a trip to the museum

Culture note ⓘ

Rome has some of the most impressive museums and archaeological sites in the world. The Vatican Museums (*Musei Vaticani*), within Vatican City, get over 4 million visitors each year. There are over 20 separate museums, palaces, galleries, and chapels, full of priceless works of art. The Sistine Chapel, with its famous ceiling painted by Michelangelo, is perhaps the most famous of these.

Video Dialog

Giulia pays a visit to the tourist information office. She is looking for some information on the local sites.

Watch the video dialog online at Active Italian: Level 2 > Unit 1 > Lesson 1 > Video dialog

Giulia:	*Buongiorno, signora. Mi può aiutare?*
Sig.ra Duranti:	*Sì?*
Giulia:	*Vorrei andare al Museo Nazionale. È lontano da qui?*
Sig.ra Duranti:	*È abbastanza lontano, sarebbe meglio prendere la metro.*
Giulia:	*Devo cambiare?*
Sig.ra Duranti:	*Sì, deve cambiare a Termini.*
Giulia:	*Dov'è la stazione della metro?*
Sig.ra Duranti:	*C'è una stazione a due minuti da qui. Uscendo da qui, è proprio lì sulla sua sinistra. Ma il museo è chiuso oggi. È lunedì.*
Giulia:	*Come?*
Sig.ra Duranti:	*Il Museo nazionale è chiuso oggi. È chiuso il lunedì.*
Giulia:	*Oh, accidenti!*

Giulia:	Hello. Can you help me?

Mrs. Duranti:	Yes?
Giulia:	I'd like to go to the National Museum. Is it far from here?
Mrs. Duranti:	It's quite far. It would be better to take the subway.
Giulia:	Do I need to change?
Mrs. Duranti:	Yes, you have to change at Termini.
Giulia:	Where's the subway station?
Mrs. Duranti:	There's a station two minutes away. When you walk out of here, it's just there on your left. But the museum is closed today. It's Monday.
Giulia:	Pardon?
Mrs. Duranti:	The National Museum is closed today. It's closed on Mondays.
Giulia:	Darn!

Grammar

....

In this section we go over some of the grammar points introduced in the dialog.

Go to Active Italian: Level 2 > Unit 1 > Lesson 1 > Grammar to listen to these explanations and to access some interactive practice activities.

1 ›   **Asking for help**

Mi può aiutare? (Can you help me?) is extremely useful when you need help of any kind.

You can go up to someone in the street with:
Scusi, mi può aiutare?

Then you can make your request.

| *Vorrei andare al duomo.* | I want to go to the cathedral. |
| *Vorrei andare alla stazione.* | I want to go to the station. |

Potere is normally followed by the infinitive form of the verb. Italian infinitives usually end in *are* (*parlare*), *-ere* (*prendere*) or *-ire* (*finire*).

2 › Going to a place

When saying where you're going, *andare* is followed by *a* and the name of the town or city: *a Roma*, *a Milano*, *a Palermo*.

If the place is introduced by *il*, *la*, *lo* or *l'*, then *a* combines with the article: *al*, *alla*, *all'* or *allo* (in the singular) and *ai*, *alle*, *agli* (in the plural).

Vado al museo.	I'm going to the museum.
Vado alla Cappella Sistina.	I'm going to the Sistine Chapel.
Vado allo stadio.	I'm going to the stadium.
Vado all'ospedale.	I'm going to the hospital.

When it is a country or continent you are going to, *andare* is
followed by *in* and the name of the country or continent:

Vado in Spagna.	I am going to Spain.
Vado in Francia.	I am going to France.
Vado in Europa.	I am going to Europe.

But you say:

negli Stati Uniti	to the United States
nel Regno Unito	to the United Kingdom

3 › **Quite, very, too, just**

Some useful words to modify adjectives include:

abbastanza	quite
È abbastanza lontano.	It's quite far.

molto	very
È molto lontano.	It's very far.

troppo	too
È troppo lontano.	It's too far.

proprio	just
È proprio di fronte.	It's just across.

These words are called adverbs and unlike many words in Italian,
adverbs always stay the same.

4 › It would be better to...

Bisogna means "it is necessary" or "you have to," but if you don't want to be quite so dogmatic, you can say *Sarebbe meglio* (It would be better). It is followed by the infinitive.

Sarebbe meglio prendere l'autobus.	It would be better to take the bus.
Sarebbe meglio andare a piedi.	It would be better to go by foot.

5 › It's Monday

When saying what day it is, just use *è*.

È lunedì.	It's Monday.
È sabato.	It's Saturday.

Oggi means "today."

Oggi è venerdì.

Today is Friday.

When you want to say that something happens regularly on a certain day, you put *il* in front of the day of the week from Monday to Saturday, and *la* in front of *domenica* (Sunday).

| È chiuso la domenica. | It is closed on Sundays. |
| Il martedì faccio la spesa. | I do my shopping on Tuesdays. |

Remember, days of the week start with a small letter in Italian.

6 › **Remember the gender!**

As you know, Italian nouns have a gender, either masculine or feminine. Try to remember the gender of nouns when you first learn them.

Il museo is a masculine word, so when Signora Duranti refers to the museum, she says *è chiuso*.

È chiuso il lunedì.

It is closed on Mondays.

As you can see, you don't need a word for "it," but you must match the ending of *chiuso* to *museo*. This is known as "agreeing."

But when talking about *la pizzeria* (pizzeria), which is a feminine noun, you would say *chiusa*.

È chiusa il lunedì.

It is closed on Mondays.

7 ›   **Agreement in the plural**

We have seen how the ending of *chiuso* has to agree with the gender of what it refers to: *il museo è chiuso*, *la pizzeria è chiusa*. If you are referring to something plural, then it also has to be reflected:

I musei sono chiusi il lunedì.	The museums are closed on Mondays.
Le pizzerie sono chiuse il lunedì.	The pizzerias are closed on Mondays.

Listening to and reading as much Italian as you can will help you become familiar with the rules of agreement.

> **Culture note** ⓘ
>
> Many museums in Italy are closed on Mondays. Always check before you plan a visit. Most towns and cities have a well-informed and helpful tourist office (*Ufficio Turistico*) in which you can ask opening times of local museums. You can also check online, in guidebooks, or at the museums for further information.
>
> Ufficio turistico
>
> Museo

 # *Vocabulary*

In this section you will learn some useful words and expressions from the dialog.

 Go to Active Italian: Level 2 > Unit 1 > Lesson 1 > Vocabulary to listen to each of the words being pronounced and to access some interactive practice activities.

aiutare
to help

Mi può aiutare?
Can you help me?

il museo
museum

Scusi, dov'è il Museo Nazionale?
Excuse me, where is the National Museum?

qui vicino
near here

È qui vicino?
Is it near here?

da lì
from there

Da lì bisogna continuare a piedi.
From there you need to continue on foot.

cambiare
to change

Bisogna cambiare treno?
Do I need to change trains?

un minuto
a minute

C'è un albergo a cinque minuti da qui.
There's a hotel five minutes from here.

uscire
to go out

Bisogna uscire da qui.
You have to go out from here.

l'uscita
exit

Dov'è l'uscita?
Where is the exit?

entrare
to enter

Bisogna entrare da lì.
You have to go in from there.

l'ingresso
admission, entrance fee

Quanto costa l'ingresso?
How much is the admission?

Culture note ⓘ

When visiting churches you should dress appropriately with shoulders covered and long pants. There are often signs before entering to remind you of this, along with other warnings advising you not to use cameras or to use them only without a flash. Remember that they are primarily places of worship.

UNIT 1 › LESSON 2
Getting directions to a museum

Italy boasts some of the greatest Renaissance artists: Titian (*Tiziano*), Michelangelo, and Leonardo da Vinci. Works of art by Italian Renaissance masters can be found in all major Italian cities, situated in the main squares, churches, and museums. Many towns exhibit pieces by the artists that came from the local region or worked in the area.

An example of this is the great number of Titian's work found in Venice, where the artist lived and worked.

Some of the best-known Italian masterpieces include Michelangelo's Last Judgement (*il Giudizio universale*), found in the Sistine Chapel (*la Cappella Sistina*) in St. Peter's Basilica, Rome, David (*David*), the original sculpture found in the Galleria dell'Accademia in Florence, Leonardo da Vinci's Last Supper (*L'Ultima cena*, also known as *il Cenacolo*) that is found inside Santa Maria delle Grazie, a church in Milan and the Mona Lisa (*La Gioconda*) found in the Louvre, Paris.

Video Dialog

· ·

The tourist office assistant, Signora Duranti, recommends the Civic Museum where there is an exhibition on the work of Giulia's favorite artist.

 Italian: Level 2 > Unit 1 > Lesson 2 > Video dialog

Sig.ra Duranti:	*Vada al Museo Civico, è aperto il lunedì.*
Giulia:	*Che cosa c'è in questo museo?*
Sig.ra Duranti:	*Ci sono molte opere del Rinascimento.*
Giulia:	*Adoro il Rinascimento.*
Sig.ra Duranti:	*In questo momento c'è una mostra meravigliosa su Raffaello.*
Giulia:	*Raffaello è il mio artista preferito!*
Sig.ra Duranti:	*Prenda l'autobus: se prende il 24 non deve cambiare.*
Giulia:	*Dov'è la fermata dell'autobus?*
Sig.ra Duranti:	*Continui sempre dritto per questa strada, giri a destra e la fermata dell'autobus è sulla sua sinistra.*
Giulia:	*Grazie mille, signora.*
Sig.ra Duranti:	*Non c'è di che.*

· ·

Mrs. Duranti:	Go to the Civic Museum, it's open on Mondays.
Giulia:	What is there in this museum?
Mrs. Duranti:	There are a lot of Renaissance works.
Giulia:	I love the Renaissance.

Mrs. Duranti:	At the moment there's a wonderful exhibition on Raphael.
Giulia:	Raphael is my favorite artist!
Mrs. Duranti:	Take the bus. If you take the number 24, you don't need to change.
Giulia:	Where's the bus stop?
Mrs. Duranti:	Continue straight along this street, turn right and the bus stop is on your left.
Giulia:	Thank you very much.
Mrs. Duranti:	Not at all.

Grammar

 Active Italian: Level 2 › Unit 1 › Lesson 2 › Grammar

8 › My, your, his, her... (1)

The word for "my" is *mio* as in *il mio artista preferito* (my favorite artist). It is a possessive adjective.

Possessive adjectives are:

mio	my
tuo	(*familiar*) your
suo	his/her/its
suo	(*formal*) your
nostro	our
vostro	(*plural*) your
loro	their

9 › | My, your, his, her... (2)

Mio (my), *tuo* (your), *suo* (his, her, its and formal your), etc.,
agree with the thing they refer to (whether it is masculine,
feminine, singular or plural) and not the person who owns it. The
article (*il*, *la*, etc.) is also usually included.

il mio albergo	my hotel
la mia casa	my house
il tuo albergo	your hotel
la tua casa	your house
il nostro albergo	our hotel
la nostra casa	our house
il vostro albergo	your hotel
la vostra casa	your house

You need to take care with *suo* as it can mean "his, her, its" or
formal "your." The situation will tell you which one it is.

Ecco, signora, il suo passaporto.	Here, madam, your passport.
Puoi dare questo a Tom? È il suo passaporto.	Can you give this to Tom? It's his passport.

"Their" is *loro*. *Loro* doesn't change.

il loro albergo	their hotel
la loro casa	their house

10 › My, your, his, her... (3)

Remember that possessive adjectives also have to agree in the plural:

i miei or *le mie*	my
i tuoi or *le tue*	(*familiar*) your
i suoi or *le sue*	his, her, its
i suoi or *le sue*	(*formal*) your
i nostri or *le nostre*	our
i vostri or *le vostre*	(*plural*) your
i loro or *le loro*	their

Dove sono le mie cose?	Where are my things?
Dove sono i nostri passaporti?	Where are our passports?
Ecco i suoi biglietti.	Here are your tickets.

11 › My favorite...

Giulia says that her favorite artist is Raphael. *Il mio artista preferito è Raffaello.*

You can use this expression for your favorite actress or singers:

La mia attrice preferita è Angelina Jolie.	My favorite actress is Angelina Jolie.
I miei cantanti preferiti sono...	My favorite singers are...

Note how you must make the words "my" and "favorite" agree with who (or what) they refer to.

Remember that Italian words ending in *-ista* can be either masculine or feminine: *il/la dentista* (dentist), *il/la ciclista* (cyclist), *l'autista* (driver), *il/la barista* (bartender), etc.

12 › Giving directions (1)

To give directions (or orders) you need a particular form of the verb.
For verbs ending in *-are* the ending is *-i*.
For verbs ending in *-ere* or *-ire* the ending is *-a*.

Continui per questa strada.	Continue down this street.
Giri a destra.	Turn right.
Prenda l'autobus.	Take the bus

Andare (to go) has a special form:

Vada al Museo Civico.
Go to the Civic Museum.

This is the polite form that you would hear if you asked someone for directions.

13 › Giving directions (2)

If Giulia was giving the same instructions to a friend, she would use the *tu* form.

For verbs ending in -*are* the ending is -*a*.
For verbs ending in -*ere* or -*ire* the ending is -*i*.

Continua per questa strada.	Continue down this street.
Gira a destra.	Turn right.
Prendi l'autobus.	Take the bus.

The form for *andare* is:

Va' al Museo Civico.
Go to the Civic Museum.

If there were more than one of you being given directions, then the *voi* form of the verb would be used:

> *Continuate*
>
> *Girate*
>
> *Prendete*

14 › **Not at all!**

Non c'è di che is another way of saying *prego* ("not at all," "don't mention it" or "you're welcome").

It is slightly more formal or emphatic than *prego*.

How to say "on the" – *su* + masculine *il*, *l'*

Another short word that combines with the article is *su* (on) and it follows the usual pattern.

In front of a masculine noun, *su* combines with *il* or *l'* to become *sul* (or *sull'*):

sul battello	on the boat
sull'aereo	on the airplane

In the plural, *su* combines with *i* to become *sui* or with *gli* to become *sugli*:

sui treni	on the trains
sugli aerei	on the airplanes

How to say "on the" – *su* + *lo*

With the *lo* article, *su* combines with *lo* to become *sullo* in the singular and *sugli* in the plural:

sullo stoino	on the doormat
sugli stoini	on the doormats

17 › How to say "on the" – *su + la*

When you use *su* in front of a feminine noun, *su* combines with *la* to become *sulla* (or *sull'*) in the singular and *sulle* in the plural:

sulla montagna	on the mountain
sull'erba	on the grass
sulle colline	on the hills

18 › A thousand thanks

A stronger alternative to *grazie* is *grazie mille* (literally "a thousand thanks").

Vocabulary

 Active Italian: Level 2 > Unit 1 > Lesson 2 > Vocabulary

la cosa
thing

Dove sono le mie cose?
Where are my things?

aperto/a
open

La posta è aperta oggi?
Is the post office open today?

chiuso/a
closed

Il ristorante è chiuso oggi.
The restaurant is closed today.

molto/a
many/much/lots of

Ci sono molte persone qui.
There are lots of people here.

l'opera
opera, (piece of) work

Mi piacciono le opere di Michelangelo.
I like the works of Michelangelo.

il Rinascimento
the Renaissance

Adoro il Rinascimento.
I love the Renaissance.

il secolo
century

Quale secolo?
Which century?

la mostra
exhibition

Quando c'è la mostra?
When is the exhibition?

la pinacoteca
art gallery

La pinacoteca è nel centro storico.
The art gallery is in the old part of town.

meraviglioso/a
wonderful

Che quadro meraviglioso!
What a wonderful painting!

la statua
statue

Chi raffigura questa statua?
Who is this statue of?

a destra
to/on the right

Bisogna girare a destra.
You have to turn right.

a sinistra
to/on the left

Giri a sinistra.
Turn left.

Culture note ⓘ

Once your bus or subway ticket has been date stamped, it is usually valid for a number of minutes – generally 75 minutes. If you are going to stay in a town or city for more than a couple of days, investigate the different  travel cards. A *carta turistica* allows unlimited travel. Ask at the tourist office (*Ufficio Turistico*) for further information.

2

Lesson 1: Asking the way to the stadium

» The conditional tense and corresponding verb endings: *-ei, -esti, -ebbe, -emmo, -este, -ebbero*.
» How to say which team you support: *Faccio il tifo per...*
» Simple expressions: *Bisogna...* and *Basta...*
» How to use *per* and *da*: *un treno per Roma, un aereo da Londra*.
» Expressions with *avere*: *aver tempo di, aver fame, aver sete*, etc.
» How to say "at" a time and "from" a time: *alle .../dalle...*

Lesson 2: A quick beer before the soccer game

» How to switch from formal *lei* to friendly *tu*: *darsi del tu*.
» The present tense of *dare*.
» The expression *aver bisogno di*.
» Different ways of saying "yes."
» Using *che* in expressions such as *Che bella casa!*

C Collins | Livemocha™

UNIT 2 › LESSON 1

Asking the way to the stadium

Culture note ⓘ

The *Stadio Olimpico* in Rome is Italy's second biggest stadium after the San Siro in Milan and can seat over 72,000 people. It staged athletics events in the 1960 Olympic Games and continues to host international athletic meetings as well as concerts. The stadium is also shared by the soccer teams Roma and Lazio.

Video Dialog

Michele asks Ugo for directions and surprises him with a generous offer.

 Active Italian: Level 2 > Unit 2 > Lesson 1 > Video dialog

Michele:	*Mi scusi! Vorrei andare allo stadio Olimpico. È lontano?*
Ugo:	*Ehm... sì. Bisogna prendere la metro, la linea B. Bisogna cambiare a Termini e prendere la linea A per tre fermate. Da lì è facile, basta seguire i cartelli per lo stadio. Va alla partita di stasera?*
Michele:	*Sì, faccio il tifo per il Milan. Veramente, ho due biglietti. Il mio amico non può venire stasera. Vuole venirci lei?*
Ugo:	*Volentieri! A che ora comincia la partita?*
Michele:	*Alle diciannove e trenta.*
Ugo:	*Che ore sono adesso?*
Michele:	*Ehm, sono le sei e un quarto.*
Ugo:	*Bene, abbiamo tempo di bere qualcosa. Offro io.*

Michele:	Excuse me. I'd like to go the Olympic stadium. Is it far?
Ugo:	Er... yes. You have to take the subway, line B. You have to change at Termini and then take line A for three stops. From there it is easy, all you have to do is follow the signs to the stadium. Are you going to the game tonight?

Michele:	Yes, I support Milan. Actually I have two tickets. My friend can't come this evening. Would you like to come?
Ugo:	Gladly! What time does the game begin?
Michele:	At 7:30.
Ugo:	What time is it now?
Michele:	Er... it's a quarter past six.
Ugo:	Good, we've time for a drink. It's on me.

Grammar

· ·

Active Italian: Level 2 > Unit 2 > Lesson 1 > Grammar

1 › **The conditional tense**

To ask politely for something or to express a wish, the conditional tense of *volere* (to want) is used. So *vorrei* (I would like) rather than the present tense *voglio* (I want) is used.

We have encountered it before in the expressions *sarebbe meglio* (it would be better to), *potrebbe* (you could), and *potremmo* (we could).

To make different tenses in Italian, you add different endings to the stem of the verb. For *volere*, the conditional stem is *vorr-*.

Here is the conditional tense:

vorrei	I would like
vorresti	you (familiar) would like
vorrebbe	he/she/it would like
vorrebbe	you (formal) would like
vorremmo	we would like
vorreste	you (plural) would like
vorrebbero	they would like

The conditional tense endings are the same for *all* verbs.

2 › **Asking a question**

Remember that asking a question is simple. You don't need to change the word order of a statement, just raise the pitch of your voice in a questioning manner.

Va alla partita di stasera.	You are going to this evening's game.
Va alla partita di stasera?	Are you going to this evening's game?

3 › Simple expressions

Two useful expressions are: *Bisogna* (literally "It is necessary to") and *Basta* (literally "It is enough to"). They often translate as "We/You need to" or "All you have to do is." Both expressions are followed by the infinitive form of the verb.

Bisogna prendere la metropolitana.	You need to take the subway.
Basta seguire i cartelli.	All you have to do is follow the signs.

4 › It is easy/difficult

Other simple but useful phrases are:
È facile (It is easy) and its opposite *È difficile* (It is difficult). Again, they are followed by the infinitive form of the verb.

È facile parlare l'italiano.	It is easy to speak Italian.
È difficile parlare l'inglese.	It is difficult to speak English.

5 › **Making negative statements**

Instead of *È difficile* (It is difficult) you could simply say *Non è facile* (It isn't easy).

To make a negative statement, put *non* in front of the verb

Il mio amico non può venire.	My friend can't come.
Il mio orologio non funziona.	My watch isn't working.
Non vorrebbe perdere la partita.	He wouldn't want to miss the game.

6 › **The words *per* (for, to) and *da* (from)**

Ugo tells Michele to follow the signs *per lo stadio* (to the stadium). *Per*, meaning "for," is used to indicate a destination. You use *per* when asking for a train, plane or ticket to somewhere.

Questo è il treno per Roma?	Is this the train to Rome?
L'aereo per Londra parte alle nove.	The plane to London leaves at 9.
Un biglietto per Como, per favore.	A ticket to Como, please.

When talking about where a train or plane is coming from, you use *da* (from).

Questo è il treno da Roma?
Is this the train from Rome?

L'aereo da Londra arriva alle venti.
The airplane from London arrives at 8 p.m.

Remember that *andare* (to go) is followed by *a* for places, towns, and cities, and *in* for countries and continents.

Vado a Roma.	I am going to Rome.
Andiamo in Italia.	We are going to Italy.

7 › **Avere (to have) in different expressions**

Avere (to have) is used in a number of set expressions, including:

avere tempo di	to have time to
Non ho tempo di mangiare.	I don't have time to eat.
avere sete	to be thirsty
Ho molta sete.	I am very thirsty.

avere fame	to be hungry
Non ho molta fame.	I'm not very hungry.
avere... anni	to be... years old
Ho ventidue anni.	I am 22 years old.
avere caldo	to be hot
Ho molto caldo.	I am very hot.
avere freddo	to be cold
Ho molto freddo.	I am very cold.

8 › **Alle + the time**

Ugo asks Michele when the soccer game begins.

> *A che ora comincia la partita?*

Michele replies

> *Alle sette e mezza.*
> At 7:30.

Note the use of *alle* meaning "at." It is always *alle* except when referring to one o'clock, when it is *all'una*.

Alle comes from combining *a* with the article *le* of *le ore* (the hours).

| *La partita comincia alle sette e mezza.* | The game begins at 7:30 p.m. |
| *Il film finisce alle dieci.* | The movie finishes at 10 p.m. |

9 › *Dalle* + the time

We have already come across *da* meaning "from." It is also used with time and works much the same way as *alle*. To say "from" a particular time it is *dalle*, except for one o'clock, when it is *dall'una*.

| *dall'una e mezza* | from one thirty |
| *dalle nove* | from nine o'clock |

Il negozio è aperto dalle nove alle sei.
The shop is open from 9 to 6.

Vocabulary

 Active Italian: Level 2 > Unit 2 > Lesson 1 > Vocabulary

fare il tifo per
to be a fan/supporter of

Per chi fai il tifo?
Who do you support?

da lì
from there

Da lì bisogna continuare a piedi.
From there you have to continue by foot.

qui
here

Vieni qui da me.
Come here to me.

là
there

Vorrei quello là.
I'd like that one there.

cominciare
to start, to begin

A che ora comincia il film?
When does the movie start?

finire
to finish

A che ora finisce il film?
When does the movie finish?

adesso
now

Che cosa facciamo adesso?
What shall we do now?

dopo
later

Ti telefono dopo.
I'll phone you later.

avere tempo di
to have time to

Non ho tempo di mangiare.
I don't have time to eat.

il biglietto
ticket

Vorrei comprare due biglietti per la partita.
I'd like to buy two tickets for the game.

Culture note ⓘ

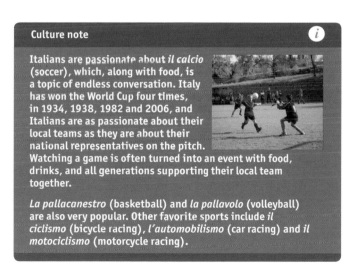

Italians are passionate about *il calcio* (soccer), which, along with food, is a topic of endless conversation. Italy has won the World Cup four times, in 1934, 1938, 1982 and 2006, and Italians are as passionate about their local teams as they are about their national representatives on the pitch. Watching a game is often turned into an event with food, drinks, and all generations supporting their local team together.

La pallacanestro (basketball) and *la pallavolo* (volleyball) are also very popular. Other favorite sports include *il ciclismo* (bicycle racing), *l'automobilismo* (car racing) and *il motociclismo* (motorcycle racing).

UNIT 2 › LESSON 2

A quick beer before the soccer game

Culture note

When you ask for a *birra* in Italy, you will be served lager. *Una birra media* is just under a pint. *Una birra piccola* is half a pint. Italian beers are known as *birre nazionali*. If you want ale or bitter, you should ask for *birra scura* (literally "dark beer") or *birra rossa* (literally "red beer").

Video Dialog

....

Ugo and Michele introduce themselves properly.

Active Italian: Level 2 > Unit 2 > Lesson 2 > Video dialog

Ugo:	*Che cosa prende?*
Michele:	*Una birra alla spina, per favore. Michele. Possiamo darci del tu, no?*
Ugo:	*Certo. Io sono Ugo. Che cosa fai nella vita, Michele?*
Michele:	*Sono fotografo.*
Ugo:	*Che coincidenza! Ho giusto bisogno di un fotografo!*
Michele:	*E tu che lavoro fai?*
Ugo:	*Lavoro in un'agenzia immobiliare. Due birre medie alla spina, per favore.*
Waiter:	*Subito!*

....

Ugo:	What are you having?
Michele:	A draft beer, please. I'm Michele. Can we use "tu" with each other?
Ugo:	Of course. My name is Ugo. What is it you do, Michele?
Michele:	I'm a photographer.
Ugo:	What a coincidence! A photographer is just what I'm needing!
Michele:	And what do you do?
Ugo:	I work in real estate. Two pints of draft beer, please.
Waiter:	Right away!

Grammar

· ·

Active Italian: Level 2 > Unit 2 > Lesson 2 > Grammar

1 ›   **Being less formal**

The expression *darsi del tu* means to use *tu* with each other. The verb *dare* means "to give."

Possiamo darci del tu, no?

We can use *tu* with each other, can't we?

Ugo and Michele start the conversation with the more formal *lei* form but once they've introduced themselves Michele suggests that they switch to the more friendly *tu* form.

2 › **The verb *dare* (to give)**

The verb *dare* (to give) is another irregular verb.

Here is the present tense:

do	I give
dai	you (*familiar*) give
dà	he/she/it gives
dà	you (*formal*) give
diamo	we give
date	you (*plural*) give
danno	they give

Note how *dà* has an accent on it. This tells you not only to stress the letter but it also distinguishes it from the word *da* (from).

3 › **Accents**

Accents on letters indicate that the letter should be stressed. Accents also help distinguish words that are spelled the same but have different meanings.

These include:

è - e	is – and
dà - da	gives – from
tè - per te	tea – for you

4 ›
Saying what you do

As well as saying *Sono fotografo* you can also say *Faccio il fotografo* for "I am a photographer."

Sono agente immobiliare
or
Faccio l'agente immobiliare.
I am a real estate agent.

Note that you include the definite article *il, la* or *l'* with *Faccio,* but you don't need anything with *Sono*.

5 ›
Ho bisogno di – I need

Another expression using *avere* is *avere bisogno di*, literally "to have need of."

Ho proprio bisogno di un fotografo.	I really need a photographer.
Ho bisogno di un paio di calzini.	I need a pair of socks.
Ho bisogno di un consiglio.	I need some advice.

Bisogno is always followed by *di* (or *d'*) and a noun or the verb in the infinitive.

Ho bisogno di un taxi.	I need a taxi.
Ho bisogno di bere qualcosa.	I need something to drink.

6 › **Different ways of saying yes**

We have come across a number of ways of saying yes, without using the word *sì*.

These include:

Volentieri.	I'd love to.
Perché no?	Why not?
Certo.	Of course.

7 › **What a...!**

Che is used in exclamations to express "What a...!"

Che coincidenza!	What a coincidence!
Che bella vista!	What a beautiful view!
Che peccato!	What a shame!

8 › **How...!**

Che plus an adjective is also used to express "How...!"

Che bello!	How lovely!
Che strano!	How odd!
Che buono!	How delicious!

If you are referring to something in particular, such as *una casa* (a house), *un parco* (a park) or *dei fiori* (flowers), then you have to make the adjective agree.

> *Che bella! (casa)*
> *Che bello! (parco)*
> *Che belli! (fiori)*

9 › | **What...?**

Che is also used to ask questions.

Che cosa prendi?	What are you having?
Che ore sono?	What time is it?
Che lavoro fai?	What work do you do?/What's your job?

 # *Vocabulary*

 *Active Italian: Level 2 > Unit 2 > Lesson 2 > Vocabulary*

una birra media
a pint of beer

Una birra media per me, per favore.
A pint of beer for me, please.

alla spina
draft

Preferisci una birra alla spina o in bottiglia?
Do you prefer draft or bottled beer?

in lattina
in a can

Ha della birra in lattina?
Do you have beer in cans?

subito
right away

Vengo subito.
I'm coming right away.

la foto
photo

Ti mando le foto.
I will send you the photos.

la macchina fotografica
camera

Ho una macchina fotografica digitale.
I have a digital camera.

fare una foto
to take a photo

Mi può fare una foto?
Can you take a photo of me?

scaricare le foto
to download photos

Voglio scaricare le foto sul computer.
I want to download the photos onto the computer.

fare un lavoro
to do a job

Che lavoro fai?
What job do you do?

qualcosa
something

Facciamo qualcosa?
Shall we do something?

Culture note ⓘ

In Italy, when drinking with a group of friends, each person tends to pay for their own drink unless someone offers to pay – *offro io* (it's on me). You might also hear the instruction *Lasci stare* (or *Lascia stare* among friends) which means "Leave it," in other words "Leave it, I'll pay."

3

Lesson 1: Where to go shopping?

» How word endings *-ino* and *-ina* make things
small: *piantina, piccolino.*

» Different types of shopping: *fare spese* and
fare la spesa.

» Using *fino a* with directions and time.

» How to form past participles: *comprato,
venduto, finito.*

» Ordinal numbers: *primo, secondo,* etc.

Lesson 2: Catching the bus to
the shops

» Using *-iamo* ending to make suggestions:
Let's...

» How to use *tutto* and *ogni.*

» About non-native Italian words: *sport, email,* etc.

» How to tell someone not to do something.

» How quantities are followed by *di* or *d'.*

      ○ Collins | Livemocha™

UNIT 3 › LESSON 1

Where to go shopping?

Culture note

Mi dica pure is a formal expression you often hear in tourist offices, shops, and hotels. It means "Can I help you?" (Literally "Please tell me"). *Dica* is from the verb *dire* (to say/tell).

Video Dialog

Giulia returns to the tourist information office – this time she needs to know how to find the shops.

 Active Italian: Level 2 > Unit 3 > Lesson 1 > Video dialog

Giulia:	*Buongiorno.*
Sig.ra Duranti:	*Buongiorno, mi dica pure.*
Giulia:	*Ha una piantina della città, per favore?*
Sig.ra Duranti:	*No, mi dispiace, sono finite. Dove vorrebbe andare?*
Giulia:	*Vorrei fare spese.*
Sig.ra Duranti:	*Allora vada in via Cavour.*
Giulia:	*Via Cavour? Dov'è?*
Sig.ra Duranti:	*Vada dritto fino al semaforo e poi giri a sinistra. Continui per il corso fino al primo incrocio...*
Giulia:	*È lontano?*
Sig.ra Duranti:	*Sì, è abbastanza lontano. È a piedi?*
Giulia:	*Sì.*

. . . .

Giulia:	Good morning.
Mrs. Duranti:	Good morning. Can I help you?
Giulia:	Have you got a city map, please?
Mrs. Duranti:	No. I'm sorry. We've run out. Where would you like to go?

Giulia:	I'd like to go shopping.
Mrs. Duranti:	Then go to via Cavour.
Giulia:	Via Cavour? Where is it?
Mrs. Duranti:	Go straight on as far as the traffic lights and then turn left. Carry on down the boulevard to the first intersection...
Giulia:	Is it a long way?
Mrs. Duranti:	Yes, it's quite far. Are you on foot?
Giulia:	Yes.

Grammar

 Active Italian: Level 2 > Unit 3 > Lesson 1 > Grammar

1 › **Word endings -*ino* and -*ina***

Right from the start of learning Italian, we have seen how word endings give lots of information. Endings often tell you whether a word is masculine or feminine; whether it is singular or plural; and with verbs, the endings tell you who is carrying out the verb action.

We encountered the ending -*issimo* or -*issima* that implies "very": *bello* is "beautiful" and *bellissimo* is "very beautiful."

The ending -*ino* or -*ina* means something is small. Giulia asks for a town plan or a little map, *una piantina*. *Una pianta* would be a bigger map, not quite as handy as *una piantina*.

You come across this ending frequently:

Piccolo means "small," *piccolino* means "tiny."

Tavolo means "table," *tavolino* means "little table" like the ones outside a bar.

Un cucchiaio means "spoon," *cucchiaino* means "teaspoon."

2 › Different types of shopping

There is a subtle difference between *fare la spesa* and *fare spese*.

Fare la spesa means "doing the shopping," as in the regular food shopping (a necessity).

Fare spese means shopping as in "going shopping," for more out-of-the-ordinary items such as clothes, etc.

Italians also say *fare shopping*. Again this implies something enjoyable rather than a chore.

Note that the article for *shopping* is *lo*, because of the rule about *lo* being used with words that begin with *s* + consonant (in this case the consonant is *h*).

3 › Up to or until

Fino a means "up to," "as far as," or "until."

Vada dritto fino al semaforo.
Go straight on as far as the traffic lights.

Remember that the word *a* combines with the article:

fino alla stazione	as far as the station
fino allo stadio	as far as the stadium
fino ai giardini pubblici	as far as the public gardens

Fino a is also used in expressions of time:

fino all'una	until 1 o'clock
fino alle quattro	until 4 o'clock
fino a mezzanotte	until midnight

4 › How to form past participles: finished, sold, bought.

When Giulia asks for a city map (*una piantina*), Signora Duranti replies:

No, mi dispiace, sono finite.
No, I'm sorry, they're finished.

Although she didn't actually say "The maps are finished," we know she is referring to them because of the feminine ending on *finite*.

Finito means "finished" and comes from the verb *finire* (to finish). It is known as a past participle. The rules for forming the past participle for regular verbs are straightforward.

With regular verbs ending in -*are*, such as *comprare* (to buy), you remove the -*are* and replace it with -*ato*:

> *comprato*   bought

With regular verbs ending in -*ere* such as *vendere* (to sell), you remove the -*ere* and replace it with -*uto*:

> *venduto*   sold

With regular verbs ending in -*ire* such as *finire* (to finish), you remove the -*ire* and replace it with -*ito*:

> *finito*   finished

5 › ## More on past participles

When you use a past participle with *è* (is) or *sono* (are), it acts like an adjective and must agree with the word it refers to.

In *sono finite*, *finite* is agreeing with the maps (*le piantine*).

Here are some examples:

La casa è venduta.	The house is sold.
I biglietti sono venduti.	The tickets are sold.

6 › ## Past participles and irregular verbs

Although Italian has very regular rules for verbs, not all verbs are regular.

And not all verbs are irregular all of the time. In the present tense a verb can be regular, but in other tenses it might deviate from the rule. Fortunately good dictionaries point this out and you will always be able to check.

A couple of irregular past participles that we have been using are *chiuso* (closed) from *chiudere* (to close) and *aperto* (open) from *aprire* (to open). Another is *preso* (taken) from *prendere* (to take).

The past participle of *essere* (to be) is *stato*.
The past participle of *avere* (to have) is *avuto*.
The past participle of *andare* (to go) is *andato*.

Once you become familiar with Italian, even irregularities have their own pattern and you can often make an educated guess!

7 › Cardinal and ordinal numbers

Il primo incrocio is "the first intersection." We have already come across the numbers *uno, due, tre, quattro* and so on. These are known as cardinal numbers.

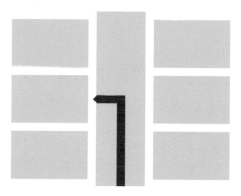

First, second, third, and so on, are ordinal numbers as they put things in order.

Ordinal numbers agree with the word they are putting in order:

la prima casa	the first house
la seconda strada	the second street
i primi fiori	the first flowers

8 › Ordinal numbers

The ordinal numbers from first to tenth are:

primo/a	first
secondo/a	second
terzo/a	third
quarto/a	fourth
quinto/a	fifth
sesto/a	sixth
settimo/a	seventh
ottavo/a	eighth
nono/a	ninth
decimo/a	tenth

When written with a figure, they are normally followed by a tiny superscript *o* for masculine things (1°, 2°) and a tiny superscript *a* for feminine things (1ª, 2ª).

Vocabulary

....

Active Italian: Level 2 > Unit 3 > Lesson 1 > Vocabulary

sto cercando
I'm looking for

Sto cercando il Municipio.
I'm looking for the city hall.

la strada
street, road

Bisogna prendere la prima strada a sinistra.
You have to take the first road on the left.

andare dritto
to go straight

Devi andare dritto fino al duomo.
You have to go straight until the cathedral.

l'incrocio
intersection

Continua fino al secondo incrocio.
Keep going until the second intersection.

la rotonda
traffic circle

Quando arrivi alla rotonda, prendi la prima uscita.
When you get to the traffic circle, take the first exit.

il semaforo
traffic lights

Bisogna spegnere il motore al semaforo.
You need to turn your engine off at the traffic lights.

a sinistra
to/on the left

La banca è a sinistra.
The bank is on the left.

a destra
to/on the right

Per evitare la galleria prendi la strada a destra.
To avoid the tunnel, take the road on the right.

in questa zona
in this area

C'è una pizzeria in questa zona?
Is there a pizzeria in this area?

il parcheggio
parking lot

È aperto il parcheggio?
Is the parking lot open?

l'autostrada
highway

L'autostrada è chiusa a causa di un incidente.
The highway is closed because of an accident.

l'uscita
highway exit

Per andare a Venezia, bisogna prendere la prossima uscita.
To go to Venice, you have to take the next exit.

il centro commerciale
shopping mall

Il centro commerciale è proprio di fronte all'aeroporto.
The shopping mall is right across from the airport.

Culture note

Mi dispiace means "I am sorry."

If someone approaches you in the street for directions and you are not able to help them, you can say *Mi dispiace, non lo so* (I am sorry, I don't know).

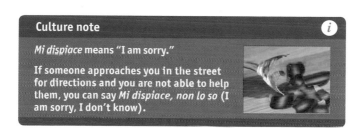

UNIT 3 › LESSON 2

Catching the bus to the shops

Culture note

A single subway ticket is generally valid for 75 minutes (from time of stamping or validation) and can often be used for one subway ride and any number of bus and tram journeys within that time limit.

There are also 10-journey tickets (*un biglietto da dieci corsi*) that need to be validated each time you make a trip. Check at the tourist office to find out about the best deals on public transportation.

It is important to remember to validate your ticket before getting on the bus or train. There are small yellow boxes at the start of train station platforms or in train stations in which you can stamp your ticket before getting on a train. For travel by bus, although you can buy tickets on some buses, it's always best to check and purchase one beforehand if possible. You can usually buy tickets in the local *tabaccheria* (tobacconist store selling stamps, postcards, candy, and tickets for local transportation). Remember to stamp your ticket when you get on the bus.

Video Dialog

Signora Duranti gives Giulia some helpful directions.

 Active Italian: Level 2 > Unit 3 > Lesson 2 > Video dialog

Sig.ra Duranti:	*Allora prenda l'autobus.*
Giulia:	*È frequente il servizio?*
Sig.ra Duranti:	*Ehm, vediamo... l'orario degli autobus... Ecco: prenda il 10, passa ogni dieci minuti.*
Giulia:	*Dove devo scendere?*
Sig.ra Duranti:	*L'autobus ferma proprio di fronte ai negozi.*
Giulia:	*Dove posso comprare il biglietto?*
Sig.ra Duranti:	*Può comprare un blocchetto di 10 biglietti in una tabaccheria o in un'edicola.Costa 12 euro. Altrimenti può comprare un biglietto solo,ma è più caro.E non si dimentichi di timbrare il biglietto quando sale sull'autobus.*
Giulia:	*Grazie mille, signora.*
Sig.ra Duranti:	*Di nulla, buona giornata.*

Mrs. Duranti:	Take the bus, then.
Giulia:	Is the service frequent?

Mrs. Duranti:	Er, let's see... the bus schedule... Here it is: take the number 10. It goes every 10 minutes.
Giulia:	Where do I have to get off?
Mrs. Duranti:	The bus stops right opposite the shops.
Giulia:	Where can I buy a ticket?
Mrs. Duranti:	You can get a book of 10 at a tobacconist's or at a newsstand. It costs 12 euros. Otherwise you can buy just one ticket, but it's more expensive. And don't forget to stamp your ticket when you board the bus.
Giulia:	Thanks very much.
Mrs. Duranti:	Don't mention it. Have a good day.

 # *Grammar*

....

Active Italian: Level 2 > Unit 3 > Lesson 2 > Grammar

1 › **So...**

Allora means "so" or "then." It is often used when you are
thinking about what you are going to say next.

2 ›   Let's see...

Vediamo means "Let's see."

The *noi* form which ends in *-iamo* is what you use to make suggestions to one or more people.

Andiamo in piscina.	Let's go to the swimming pool.
Compriamo dei panini.	Let's buy some sandwiches.
Andiamo a piedi.	Let's walk.

3 ›   All and every...

The words *ogni* and *tutto* mean "all" or "every," depending on the context. *Ogni* is invariable and never changes. You don't use the article (*il*, *la*, *lo*, etc.) with it.

ogni giorno	every day
ogni settimana	every week
ogni dieci minuti	every ten minutes

Tutto, however, has to agree with the word it goes with and is followed by the article *il, la, lo*, etc.

tutto il pane	all the bread
tutti i negozi	all the stores
tutti i giorni	every day
tutta la gente	all the people
tutte le agenzie	all the agencies

4 › Non-native words

All Italian nouns end in *-o, -a, -i* or *-e*. Anything else you find is non-native!

The thing to remember about these words is that they don't change in the plural. Remember, though, that the article does.

l'autobus	*gli autobus*
il tram	*i tram*
lo sport	*gli sport*
il bar	*i bar*

Most non-native words are masculine. A few, such as *email* and *password*, are feminine.

Ho ricevuto la tua email.	I received your email.
Qual è la tua password?	What is your password?

5 › Plural of nouns ending in *-io*

The plural of most masculine nouns ending in *-io* is *-i* and not *-ii*.

l'orario – gli orari	timetable
il negozio – i negozi	store
lo studio – gli studi	study

Occasionally a plural will end in double *i*. It happens when the stress falls on the final *i* as in *lo zio*. The plural is therefore *gli zi**i***.

6 › 　Instructions not to do something

The lady in the tourist office tells Giulia not to forget to stamp (validate) her bus ticket.

> *Non si dimentichi di timbrare il biglietto.*
>
> Don't forget to stamp your ticket.

To tell someone not to do something using the polite *lei* form is simple, you just place *non* in front of the verb.

Non compri questo formaggio.	Don't buy this cheese.
Non vada a piedi. È lontano.	Don't go by foot. It is far.
Non scenda qui.	Don't get off here.

If you are using the *tu* form then *non* is followed by the infinitive.

> *Non comprare questo formaggio.*
> *Non andare a piedi.*
> *Non scendere qui.*

7 › Quantities followed by *di*

The lady in the tourist office advises Giulia to buy a book of 10 tickets, *un blocchetto di 10 biglietti*.

When talking about quantities such as a glass of, a bottle of, a bit of, a liter of, and so on, "of" is *di* or *d'* and not *del, della, dei* and so on.

Un bicchiere di vino.	A glass of wine.
Una bottiglia d'acqua minerale.	A bottle of mineral water.
Un po' di burro.	A bit of butter.
Un litro di latte.	A liter of milk.

Vocabulary

fuori servizio
out of order

Il bancomat e fuori servizio.
The ATM is out of order.

passare
to go by

Ogni quanto passa l'autobus?
How often do the buses go by?

l'orario
schedule

Ha l'orario dei battelli?
Do you have the boat schedule?

fermare
to stop

L'autobus ferma di fronte al museo.
The bus stops opposite the museum.

un blochetto di 10 biglietti
a book of 10 tickets

Vuole un biglietto di corsa singola o un blochetto di 10 biglietti?
Do you want a single ticket or a book of 10 tickets?

la tabaccheria
tobacco shop

Cerco una tabaccheria.
I'm looking for a tobacco shop.

un'edicola
newsstand

C'è un'edicola in Piazza Cavour.
There is a newsstand in Piazza Cavour.

la fermata
stop

Non scendere qui. Questa non è la tua fermata.
Don't get off here. This isn't your stop.

salire sull'autobus
to get on the bus

Quando sali sull'autobus devi timbrare il biglietto.
When you get on the bus you have to validate your ticket.

davanti a
in front of, opposite

La fermata dell'autobus é davanti al centro commerciale.
The bus stop is opposite the shopping mall.

Culture note

City buses are generally orange. You usually enter from the rear and stamp your ticket in the machine as you enter. If the bus is very crowded, you can say either *scusi* or *permesso* to get past people. If there is no way of reaching the validating machine, hand your ticket to someone nearer the machine who will do it for you.

4

Lesson 1: In the clothes shop

» How to ask for different items of clothing.

» How to talk about different sizes: *piccola*, *media*, *grande*.

» How to describe different colors.

» How to say whether they fit or not: *mi va benissimo*.

» How to use object pronouns: *lo, la, li, le*.

» How to ask how much something is.

Lesson 2: A little black dress

» How to say you are doing something using *stare: sto cercando*.

» How to say you want something special: *qualcosa di speciale*.

» How to make a negative construction using *non... niente*.

» How to ask if you can pay by credit card.

» How to form the imperfect tense: *costava*.

C Collins | Livemocha™

UNIT 4 › LESSON 1

In the clothes shop

Culture note ⓘ

In Italy you should always say *buongiorno* or *buona sera* to the staff when you enter a store and use the *lei* (you, formal) form, even if the staff are very young. Using *tu* to a salesclerk is considered rude.

Video Dialog

Giulia goes on the hunt for some new clothes.

 Active Italian: Level 2 > Unit 4 > Lesson 1 > Video dialog

Giulia:	*Buongiorno.*
Lucia:	*Buongiorno, desidera?*
Giulia:	*Vorrei una maglia rossa, taglia media.*
Lucia:	*Ecco, questa è una taglia 44.*
Giulia:	*Grazie, ma è troppo grande.*
Lucia:	*Provi questa.*
Giulia:	*È bella, ma è troppo piccola.*
Lucia:	*Allora provi una 42.*
Giulia:	*Ah sì, grazie. Mi va benissimo. Quanto costa?*
Lucia:	*49 euro.*
Giulia:	*Perfetto, la prendo. Posso pagare con la carta di credito?*
Lucia:	*Certo.*

Giulia:	Good morning.
Lucia:	Good morning, what would you like?
Giulia:	I would like a red sweater, medium size.
Lucia:	Here you are. This is a size 44.
Giulia:	Thank you, but it's too big.
Lucia:	Try this one.
Giulia:	It's nice but it's too small.
Lucia:	Then try a 42.

Giulia:	Yes, thanks. It fits very well. How much does it cost?
Lucia:	49 euros.
Giulia:	Perfect, I'll take it. Can I pay by credit card?
Lucia:	Of course.

Grammar

 Active Italian: Level 2 > Unit 4 > Lesson 1 > Grammar

1 › Colors

Giulia asks for a red sweater – *una maglia rossa*.
Red is *rosso*. As with most other adjectives in Italian, the color comes *after* the noun and agrees with what it is describing, in this case feminine *maglia*.

Generally a masculine adjective ending in *-o* changes to *-a* to make it feminine. In the plural, masculine adjectives end in *-i* and feminine ones in *-e*.

il cappello rosso	the red hat
la maglia rossa	the red sweater
i cappelli rossi	the red hats
le maglie rosse	the red sweaters

Normally adjectives ending in *-e* can be both masculine and feminine in the singular. In the plural, the ending (for both masculine and feminine) changes to *-i*.

il cappello verde	the green hat
la maglia verde	the green sweater
i cappelli verdi	the green hats
le maglie verdi	the green sweaters

2 › Different colors

Common colors include:

rosso	red
bianco	white
nero	black
giallo	yellow
grigio	gray
verde	green
arancio	orange
marrone (plural *marrone* or *marroni*)	brown
azzurro	blue
blu	blue
rosa	pink

Generally speaking, *azzurro* is a lighter blue than *blu*. You would use *azzurro* to describe a blue sky (*un cielo azzurro*).

3 › Colors that never change

The colors *blu* (blue), *arancio* (orange) and *rosa* (pink) are invariable, i.e. they never change. Other colours that are invariable are *beige* (beige), *viola* (purple), *bordeaux* (crimson) and *lilla* (lilac).

una camicia rosa	a pink shirt
i pantaloni rosa	pink pants
una macchina blu	a dark blue car

4 › Asking the color of something

When asking the color of something, you say: *Di che colore?*
(literally "Of what color?")

> ### *Di che colore è la macchina?*
> What color is the car?

5 › Adjectives indicating size

Useful words to do with size include:

piccolo/a	small
medio/a	medium
grande	large

una taglia media	a medium size
una taglia grande	a large size

You find Italians also use the English words: small, medium,
large, and extra large.

To qualify the size of an item of clothing you can use *troppo* (too) or *più* (more) and *meno* (less):

Questa giacca è troppo grande.	This jacket is too big.
Ha una taglia più piccola?	Do you have a smaller size?
Ha una gonna meno colorata?	Do you have a skirt that is less colorful?

6 › **Saying something fits you**

To say something fits, you use the expression *andare bene.*

Mi va benissimo.	It fits me perfectly. (literally = It goes to me very well.)
Ti va benissimo.	It fits you perfectly. (literally = It goes to you very well.)
Le va benissimo.	It fits you perfectly. (literally = It goes to you very well, using the *lei* form.)

Questa gonna mi va benissimo.	This skirt fits me perfectly.
Che bella gonna! Ti va benissimo.	What a lovely skirt! It fits you perfectly.
Signora, le va benissimo.	Madam, it fits you perfectly.

You can use a similar expression with *stare* meaning "to suit."

Mi sta benissimo.	It really suits me.
Ti sta benissimo.	It really suits you.

7 ›

Object pronouns *lo* and *la*

Pronouns are words that stand in place of a noun. In the sentence "Luisa is buying a sweater" Luisa is the subject and what she is buying (a sweater) is the object. Let's replace both subject and object with pronouns. The sentence now becomes "She is buying it." *She* is the subject pronoun replacing Luisa; *it* is the object pronoun replacing the sweater.

When Giulia says *Perfetto, la prendo* (Perfect, I'll take it), the "it" refers to the sweater (*la maglia*) and that is why it is *la*.

If she were referring to a hat (*il cappello*), she would say *Perfetto, lo prendo*.

Use *lo* to replace a masculine singular word and *la* to replace a feminine singular word.

Use *li* to replace a masculine plural word and *le* to replace a feminine plural word.

> *Perfetto, **li** prendo* (referring to *i guanti* – gloves).
> *Perfetto, **le** prendo* (referring to *le scarpe* – shoes).

8 ›   ## Asking the price

There are a number of ways of asking the price of something.

Quant'è?	How much? / How much is it?
Quanto costa?	How much does it cost?
Quanto costano?	How much do they cost?

Culture note   *i*

You will notice that fur coats and jackets or fur-lined accessories such as scarves are particularly popular in Italy. Leather and fur manufacturing is an important part of the Italian fashion production industry and these materials are commonly worn in Italy, playing a crucial part in the winter wardrobe. You'll find that it is not just those living in the mountains who wear fur, in fact many women of all ages wear fur coats or at least coats with fur-lined collars, hoods or sleeves. Men also sport coats and jackets with fur-lined hoods. Such products can be found in the popular fashion stores of Italy as well as more traditional fur specialist stores and high fashion boutiques ranging in prices and styles.

Vocabulary

· ·

Active Italian: Level 2 > Unit 4 > Lesson 1 > Vocabulary

il giubbotto
jacket

Ho freddo. Dov'è il mio giubbotto?
I'm cold. Where is my jacket?

la cintura
belt

È una cintura di pelle.
It is a leather belt.

un impermeabile
raincoat

Sta piovendo, metti l'impermeabile.
It's raining, put your raincoat on.

la maglietta
t-shirt

Che bella maglietta!
What a lovely t-shirt!

la cravatta
tie

Mio padre porta sempre la cravatta.
My father always wears a tie.

i guanti
gloves

Ha un paio di guanti?
Do you have a pair of gloves?

gli stivali
boots

C'è la neve. È meglio mettere gli stivali.
There's snow. It is better to wear boots.

i calzini
socks

Ho bisogno di un paio di calzini.
I need a pair of socks.

la gonna
skirt

La gonna è troppo stretta.
The skirt is too tight.

i pantaloni
pants

I pantaloni mi vanno bene.
The pants fit me.

UNIT 4 › LESSON 2
A little black dress

Culture note

The fashion industry is an important sector of the Italian economy and creates a large number of jobs in textile-producing areas such as Prato and Modena, where some of the world's best-known labels are based, as well as in retail. Many factories in these textile-industry regions have stores or outlets where spares, samples and slightly damaged items of designer clothing can be bought direct but at a fraction of the price.

Video Dialog

• •

Giulia continues her shopping trip and finds something nice that wasn't on her list.

 Active Italian: Level 2 > Unit 4 > Lesson 2 > Video dialog

Lucia:	*Altro?*
Giulia:	*Sì, sto cercando anche un paio di pantaloni neri.*
Lucia:	*Mi dispiace, non ho niente della sua taglia. Dei jeans?*
Giulia:	*No, grazie. Vorrei qualcosa di speciale.*
Lucia:	*Ho un vestito nero della sua taglia. È molto chic.*
Giulia:	*Posso vederlo?*
Lucia:	*Eccolo.*
Giulia:	*È perfetto. Quant'è?*
Lucia:	*È in saldo. Costava 99 euro, ma adesso costa solo 57 euro.*
Giulia:	*Lo prendo!*

· ·

Lucia:	Anything else?
Giulia:	Yes, I am also looking for a pair of black pants.
Lucia:	Sorry. I don't have anything in your size. Some jeans?
Giulia:	No thanks. I want something special.
Lucia:	I have a black dress in your size. It's very chic.
Giulia:	Can I see it?

Lucia:	Here it is.
Giulia:	It's perfect. How much is it?
Lucia:	It's on sale. It was 99 euros but now it is only 57 euros.
Giulia:	I'll take it!

Grammar

 Active Italian: Level 2 > Unit 4 > Lesson 2 > Grammar

1 › **Sto cercando... – I am looking for...**

To express an ongoing activity, use the verb *stare* (to be) and a gerund: *cercando* (looking for), *mangiando* (eating).

We've come across *stare* before in the question *Come sta?* (How are you?) and the answer *Sto bene, grazie* (I'm fine, thanks).

The present tense of *stare* is:

sto	I am
stai	you (*familiar*) are
sta	he/she/it is
sta	you (*formal*) are
stiamo	we are
state	you (*plural*) are
stanno	they are

Don't confuse *stare* with *essere* which also means "to be." Think of *stare* as a more temporary state as in:

> *Quel vestito ti sta bene.*
>
> That dress really suits you.

2 › How to form a gerund – looking, trying, finishing

To form the gerund of regular *-are* verbs, replace *-are* with *-ando*:

> *cercare* (to look for): *cerc**ando***
> *provare* (to try on): *prov**ando***

Sto cercando un paio di pantaloni neri.	I am looking for a pair of black pants.
Sto provando una giacca nera.	I am trying on a black jacket.

To form the gerund of most *-ere* and *-ire* verbs, replace *-ere* and *-ire* with *-endo*:

> *prendere* (to take): *prend**endo***
> *finire* (to finish): *fin**endo***

| *Sto prendendo un caffè.* | I am having a coffee. |
| *Il film sta finendo.* | The movie is finishing. |

3 › Something special – *qualcosa di speciale*

Qualcosa means "something."
Qualcosa followed by an adjective becomes *qualcosa di*:

| *qualcosa di speciale* | something special |
| *qualcosa di buono* | something tasty |

4 › | **Nothing or not... anything**

Non ho niente can translate "I have nothing" or "I don't have anything."

Italian has double negatives. You use both *non* and another negative word, *niente* (nothing), together.

Non ho niente nella sua taglia.	I have nothing in your size.
Non compro niente.	I'm not buying anything.

You can also use *niente* on its own:

Cosa vuoi comprare?	What do you want to buy?
Niente.	Nothing.

5 › | **Placing object pronouns**

When Lucia tells Giulia about the dress (*il vestito*), Giulia asks if she can see it: *Posso veder**lo**?*

The *lo* is replacing *il vestito*.

If they were talking about the sweater (*la maglia*), then she would say: *Posso veder**la**?*

Note how the final *-e* of the infinitive is removed before adding the *lo* or *la*: *vedere – vederlo/vederla*.

Dropping the final *-e* from the infinitive is common in Italian and makes for a smoother flow of speech.

It is also possible to place *lo* or *la* in front of *posso*:

> *Lo posso vedere?* or *Posso vederlo?*
> *La posso provare?* or *Posso provarla?*
> Can I try it on?

6 › | Imperfect tense of *-are* verbs

Lucia says that the black dress did cost 99 euros, but now it only costs 57 euros. (It is on sale.)

> *Costava 99 euro, ma adesso costa solo 57 euro.*

Costava is the imperfect tense of *costare* (to cost). The imperfect tense is used to describe what happened in the past and is often translated by "used to."

The imperfect endings for regular *-are* verbs are:

cost**avo**	I used to cost
cost**avi**	you (*familiar*) used to cost
cost**ava**	he/she/it used to cost
cost**ava**	you (*formal*) used to cost
cost**avamo**	we used to cost
cost**avate**	you (*plural*) used to cost
cost**avano**	they used to cost

7 › Imperfect tense of *-ere* verbs

The imperfect tense is also used to describe actions that
repeatedly took place in the past, as in *Andavo in Italia ogni anno*
(I went to Italy every year).

The imperfect endings for regular *-ere* verbs are:

prend**evo**	I took
prend**evi**	you (*familiar*) took
prend**eva**	he/she/it took
prend**eva**	you (*formal*) took
prend**evamo**	we took
prend**evate**	you (*plural*) took
prend**evano**	they took

8 › Imperfect tense of *-ire* verbs

The imperfect tense is also used to describe actions that were taking place when something else happened in the past, for example "I was sleeping when he phoned." *Dormivo quando ha telefonato*.

The imperfect endings for regular *-ire* verbs are:

*dorm**ivo***	I was sleeping
*dorm**ivi***	you (*familiar*) were sleeping
*dorm**iva***	he/she/it was sleeping
*dorm**iva***	you (*formal*) were sleeping
*dorm**ivamo***	we were sleeping
*dorm**ivate***	you (*plural*) were sleeping
*dorm**ivano***	they were sleeping

Vocabulary

Active Italian· level 2 > Unit 4 > Lesson 2 > Vocabulary

la camicetta
blouse

Sara ha una camicetta rosa.
Sara has a pink blouse.

la camicia da notte
nightgown

Dov'è la tua camicia da notte?
Where is your nightgown?

il pigiama
pyjamas

Dormo nudo. Non porto pigiama.
I sleep naked. I don't wear pyjamas.

la sciarpa
scarf

Metti la sciarpa. Fa freddo.
Put your scarf on. It's cold.

le scarpe da ginnastica
sneakers

Dove hai comprato le scarpe da ginnastica?
Where did you buy your sneakers?

il costume da bagno
swimsuit

Vendono costumi da bagno al mercato.
They sell swimsuits at the market.

i calzoncini
shorts

Quando ero piccolo portavo sempre i calzoncini.
When I was little I always wore shorts.

i collant
pantyhose

Fa troppo caldo per portare i collant.
It is too hot to wear pantyhose.

le mutande
underpants

Si possono comprare le mutande al supermercato.
You can buy underpants at the supermarket.

le mutandine
panties

Sono molto carine quelle mutandine.
Those panties are very pretty.

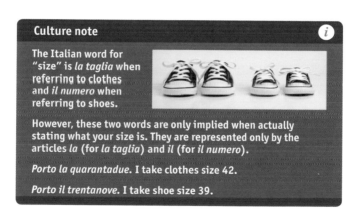

Culture note ⓘ

The Italian word for "size" is *la taglia* when referring to clothes and *il numero* when referring to shoes.

However, these two words are only implied when actually stating what your size is. They are represented only by the articles *la* (for *la taglia*) and *il* (for *il numero*).

Porto la quarantadue. I take clothes size 42.

Porto il trentanove. I take shoe size 39.

Lesson 1: In need of smart clothes

- » How to use the past tense to say what you have bought: *Ho comprato...*
- » Some common irregular past participles: *fatto, detto, preso*, etc.
- » Some irregular noun plurals: *gli uomini, le paia*, etc.
- » How to say "there": *ci*.
- » How to form the future tense: *costerà*.
- » The use of *da* in expressions such as *abiti da uomo*.
- » The use of *perché* to mean both "why?" and "because".

Lesson 2: In the men's section

- » How to shop for men's clothing.
- » How to address a group of male and female people.
- » How to describe a mix of masculine and feminine nouns.
- » How to use *più* and *meno*.
- » How to use *Che?* and *Quale?*
- » How to say what something is made of: *di plastica, di lana*, etc.
- » About the letter j in Italian.

Collins | **Livemocha™**

UNIT 5 › LESSON 1

In need of smart clothes

Culture note ⓘ

Italy offers a wide range of clothes shopping for all budgets: from designer stores to supermarkets and weekly outdoor markets. Look out for sales (*saldi*) which usually take place at the end of the summer and winter seasons. If you're in search of a bargain, try the local markets in towns and cities. They usually run on weekends and one day in the week (often Wednesdays but each city differs slightly). Bologna has a huge market that takes place every Friday and Saturday and sells a wide range of products from footwear and jewelry to fresh food and bicycles! A lot of markets have clothing that comes directly from factories where you can pick up some great deals if you shop around.

Video Dialog

· ·

Giulia shows Michele her new clothes over a coffee. Then Michele admits that he needs some new clothes himself.

 Active Italian: Level 2 > Unit 5 > Lesson 1 > Video dialog

Michele:	*E allora, che cos'hai comprato?*
Giulia:	*Ho comprato una maglia rossa e un vestito nero.*
Michele:	*Be', anch'io dovrei comprare della roba.*
Giulia:	*Perché?*
Michele:	*Perché ho una mostra fotografica a New York e non posso mica andarci con questi jeans!*
Giulia:	*Ehm... Non è proprio il look giusto!*
Michele:	*Che cosa dovrei mettermi?*
Giulia:	*Nel negozio dove ho comprato la mia maglia vendono anche abiti da uomo.*
Michele:	*Ho l'impressione che mi costerà caro!*

· ·

Michele:	So, what did you buy?
Giulia:	I bought a red sweater and a black dress.
Michele:	Well, I should buy some stuff, too.
Giulia:	Why?
Michele:	Because I'm having an exhibition of my photos in New York and I can't go there in these jeans!
Giulia:	Mmm... It isn't exactly the right image!
Michele:	What should I wear?

| Giulia: | In the shop where I bought my sweater they also sell men's clothes. |
| Michele: | I get the feeling this is going to cost me dearly! |

Grammar

....

🍥 *Active Italian: Level 2 > Unit 5 > Lesson 1 > Grammar*

1 › **How to form the past tense**

Michele asks Giulia *Che cos'hai comprato?* (What did you buy?) and Giulia begins her reply with *Ho comprato* (I bought).

To make the past tense, you use the present tense of *avere* (to have) and add the past participle which we've already learnt.

Here is a quick recap:

With most *-are* verbs, replace the *-are* with *-ato*: *comprare – comprato* (to buy – bought).

With most *-ere* verbs, replace the *-ere* with *-uto*: *vendere – venduto* (to sell – sold).

With most *-ire* verbs, replace the *-ire* with *-ito*: *finire – finito* (to finish – finished).

When you use *avere* with a past participle, *avere* is known as the auxiliary verb. It helps make the past tense. Later on you will find out that some verbs take *essere* as the auxiliary verb.

2 ›

The past tense of *comprare* (to buy)

ho comprato	I have bought
hai comprato	you (*familiar*) have bought
ha comprato	he/she/it has bought
ha comprato	you (*formal*) have bought
abbiamo comprato	we have bought
avete comprato	you (*plural*) have bought
hanno comprato	they have bought

Note how it is the auxiliary *avere* verb that changes. The past participle remains the same for each person.

Culture note ⓘ

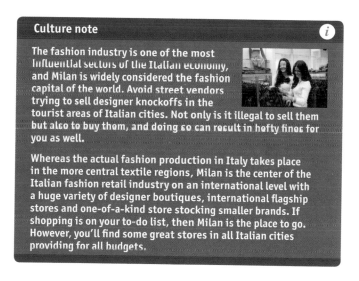

The fashion industry is one of the most influential sectors of the Italian economy, and Milan is widely considered the fashion capital of the world. Avoid street vendors trying to sell designer knockoffs in the tourist areas of Italian cities. Not only is it illegal to sell them but also to buy them, and doing so can result in hefty fines for you as well.

Whereas the actual fashion production in Italy takes place in the more central textile regions, Milan is the center of the Italian fashion retail industry on an international level with a huge variety of designer boutiques, international flagship stores and one-of-a-kind store stocking smaller brands. If shopping is on your to-do list, then Milan is the place to go. However, you'll find some great stores in all Italian cities providing for all budgets.

3 › ## Some irregular past participles

Forming a past participle does not always follow the set pattern. Here are a number of commonly used irregular ones:

prendere	to take, to catch	*preso*
fare	to do, to make	*fatto*
dire	to say	*detto*
mettere	to put on	*messo*
cuocere	to cook	*cotto*
accendere	to light	*acceso*
rispondere	to reply	*risposto*
leggere	to read	*letto*

A good dictionary will always show you these variations.

4 › ## *Perché?*

Italian uses the same word for "why" and "because." It is clear from the context which meaning applies.

Perché devi comprare della roba da vestire?	Why do you have to buy clothes?
Perché ho una mostra fotografica a New York.	Because I have an exhibition of my photos in New York.

5 › *Ci* meaning "there"

Michele says *non posso mica andarci con questi jeans!* This means he can hardly go to New York in these jeans. In Italian you have to indicate New York with the word *ci*.

Ci is a pronoun and it replaces the name of a place that has been referred to (or is implied). It is often attached to the end of *andare* minus the final -*e*: *andarci* (to go there).

Vado a New York.	I am going to New York.
Ci vado in aereo.	I am going there by plane.
Devo andarci domani.	I have to go there tomorrow.

By listening to as much Italian as you can, you will get a feel for these short but important words.

6 › *Abiti da uomo* – Men's clothing

Giulia uses the phrase *abiti da uomo*, meaning "men's clothes." The word for man is *uomo*. It has an irregular plural, *uomini*.

A number of Italian nouns have irregular plurals. A good dictionary will always flag these up.

Sometimes a noun is masculine in the singular but becomes feminine in the plural.
Un paio (a pair) is an example of this, changing from *un paio* in the singular to *le paia* in the plural.

Other nouns that behave like this include:

l'uovo (egg)	→	*le uova* (eggs)
il dito (finger)	→	*le dita* (fingers)
il braccio (arm)	→	*le braccia* (arms)
il ginocchio (knee)	→	*le ginocchia* (knees)
il lenzuolo (sheet)	→	*le lenzuola* (sheets)

7 › The use of *da*

Abiti da donna is "women's clothing."

We have already come across *da* in the following contexts:
"from" as in *il treno da Roma* (the train *from* Rome)

"from" as in *dalle nove alle sei* (*from* 9:00 to 6:00)

"to someone's place" as in *vado da Tom* (I'm going *to* Tom's) or *vado dal farmacista* (I'm going *to* the pharmacist).

In *vestiti da uomo* it is being used in its other context – that of telling you what or who something is *for*. *Da uomo* tells you the clothes are for men; *da donna* tells you they are for women; *da sera* would tell you that they would be for evening wear.

You find *da* is often used to specify what something is used for.

*una camera **da** letto*	a bedroom
*le scarpe **da** tennis*	tennis shoes, sneakers
*l'abito **da** sposa*	wedding dress

8 › **My stuff –** *la mia roba*

La roba is frequently used in Italian to mean "stuff" or "things."

> *Dove hai messo la roba da ginnastica?*
> Where have you put my gym things?

> *Dovrei comprare della roba da vestire.*
> I should buy some things to wear.

9 › **The future tense**

When Michele says *mi costerà caro* (it will cost me dearly), he uses the future of *costare – costerà*.

The future is quite simple to form. Just add the following endings.

With *-are* and *-ere* verbs, the endings are the same.

comprare – to buy

compr**erò**	I will buy
compr**erai**	you (*familiar*) will buy
compr**erà**	he/she/it will buy
compr**erà**	you (*formal*) will buy
compr**eremo**	we will buy
compr**erete**	you (*plural*) will buy
compr**eranno**	they will buy

vendere – to sell

vend**erò**	I will sell
vend**erai**	you (*familiar*) will sell
vend**erà**	he/she/it will sell
vend**erà**	you (*formal*) will sell
vend**eremo**	we will sell
vend**erete**	you (*plural*) will sell
vend**eranno**	they will sell

With most *-ire* verbs the endings are as follows:

finire – to finish

fin**irò**	I will finish
fin**irai**	you (*familiar*) will finish
fin**irà**	he/she/it will finish
fin**irà**	you (*formal*) will finish
fin**iremo**	we will finish
fin**irete**	you (*plural*) will finish
fin**iranno**	they will finish

Vocabulary

 Active Italian: Level 2 > Unit 5 > Lesson 1 > Vocabulary

accompagnare
to accompany, to go with

Ti accompagno all'ospedale.
I'll go with you to the hospital.

elegante
smart

La signora Verdi è molto elegante stasera.
Mrs. Verdi is very elegant this evening.

un completo
suit, outfit

Bisogna mettersi un completo per il matrimonio.
You have to wear a suit to the wedding.

un completo da donna
women's suit, ladies' suit

Dove posso comprare un completo da donna?
Where can I buy a ladies' suit?

l'abito da sposa
wedding dress

Andiamo a cercare un abito da sposa.
Let's go and look for a wedding dress.

le scarpe con i tacchi alti
high heeled shoes

Non mi piacciono le scarpe con i tacchi alti.
I don't like high heeled shoes.

il matrimonio
wedding, marriage

Andiamo al matrimonio di Paolo e Francesca.
We are going to Paolo and Francesca's wedding.

il grande magazzino
department store

Ci sono diversi grandi magazzini a Como.
There are several department stores in Como.

il reparto
department, section

A quale piano si trova il reparto calzature?
Which floor is the shoe department?

al primo piano
on the second floor

Il reparto biancheria intima è al primo piano.
The lingerie department is on the second floor.

il pianterreno
the first floor

Dove sei? Io sono al pianterreno.
Where are you? I am on the first floor.

al piano interrato
in the basement

C'è un piccolo supermercato al piano interrato.
There is a small supermarket in the basement.

UNIT 5 › LESSON 2

In the men's section

Video Dialog

....

Now it's Michele's turn to look for a new outfit – he needs
something for his upcoming exhibition.

Active Italian: Level 2 > Unit 5 > Lesson 2 > Video dialog

Lucia:	*Buongiorno, signori.*
Michele:	*Che cosa mi consiglia? Cerco qualcosa di un po' più elegante.*
Lucia:	*Un completo con cravatta?*
Michele:	*Qualcosa di meno formale...*
Lucia:	*Dei jeans, una dolcevita e una giacca?*
Michele:	*Sì. Ha dei jeans neri e una dolcevita nera?*
Lucia:	*Vediamo... Ecco: jeans e dolcevita.*
Michele:	*Ottimo. Che tipo di giacca mi consiglia?*
Lucia:	*Una giacca di lana o una di pelle?*
Michele:	*Una giacca di pelle.*
Lucia:	*Di che colore? Marrone o nera?*
Michele:	*Marrone se ce l'ha.*
Giulia:	*Molto chic!*

....

Lucia:	Good afternoon.
Michele:	What do you recommend? I'm looking for something a bit smarter.
Lucia:	A suit and tie?
Michele:	Something less formal...

Lucia:	Jeans, a roll neck sweater and a jacket?
Michele:	Yes. Have you some black jeans and a black roll neck sweater?
Lucia:	Let's see... Here you are: jeans and a roll neck.
Michele:	Excellent. What sort of jacket do you recommend?
Lucia:	A wool jacket or a leather one?
Michele:	A leather jacket.
Lucia:	What color? Brown or black?
Michele:	Brown if you have it.
Giulia:	Very smart!

Grammar

• •

 Active Italian: level 2 > Unit 5 > Lesson 2 > Grammar

1 › **Buongiorno, signori!**

When Giulia and Michele enter the shop, Lucia greets them with *Buongiorno, signori!* Note that she has used the masculine *signori* even though Giulia is there. This reflects what automatically happens in Italian when there is a mixture of masculine and feminine nouns (including people). Any adjectives describing them are masculine by default.

> *Max e Luisa sono alti.*
> Max and Luisa are tall.

> *La casa e il giardino sono belli.*
> The house and garden are lovely.

2 › More and less

Più means "more", *meno* means "less" and are useful to know when trying to explain what you would like.

più formale	more formal
meno formale	less formal

più caro	more expensive
meno caro	less expensive

Vorrei qualcosa di meno caro (I'd like something less expensive) sounds much less abrupt than *È troppo caro* (It is too expensive).

3 › What? and Which? (1)

Che? (What?) and *Quale?* (Which?) are two important question words. *Che* is easy because it never changes.

Che tipo di giacca vuole?
What kind of jacket do you want?

A che nome ha riservato?
Under what name is the reservation?

Che ore sono?
What time is it?

4 › **What? and Which? (2)**

While *Che?* never changes, *Quale?* shortens to *Qual* when it is followed by *è* (is).

> ### *Qual è la tua casa?*
> Which is your house?

> ### *Quale gonna vuoi comprare?*
> Which skirt do you want to buy?

Quale becomes *Quali* for plural things.

> ### *Quali pantaloni hai comprato?*
> Which pants did you buy?

> ### *Quali scarpe preferisci?*
> Which shoes do you prefer?

Quale is used when there is a choice of things and tends to be used for phone numbers, emails, and addresses, etc.

Qual è il tuo indirizzo?	What is your address?
Qual è il tuo numero di telefonino?	What is your cell phone number?
Qual è il tuo indirizzo email?	What is your email address?

5 › **Made of...**

To say what something is made of, use *di* (of) followed by the
material (wool, leather, plastic, etc).

una maglia di lana	a wool sweater
una giacca di pelle	a leather jacket
una borsa di plastica	a plastic bag
una casa di legno	a wooden house

Other materials include: *di cotone* (cotton), *di lino* (linen), *di
vetro* (glass), *di metallo* (metal), *di carta* (paper), *di seta* (silk).

6 › **Single letter words**

Italian is full of very short words. Here are the shortest:
e – and
è – is
o – or
a – at, to
i – the (masculine plural article)

7 › **The letter *j***

The Italian alphabet does not contain the letter *j* (although you find it used with foreign words that have entered the language such as *jeans*, *jeep*, and *judo*). However, the sound of the letter *j* is conveyed by *gi*. We have come across it a few times.

giacca	jacket
Giappone	Japan
Giulia	Julia
giugno	June

Vocabulary

Active Italian: Level 2 > Unit 5 > Lesson 2 > Vocabulary

di moda
fashionable

Questi pantaloni sono molto di moda.
These pants are very fashionable.

classico/a
classic

Cerco un completo classico.
I am looking for a classic suit.

a righe
striped

Ha un paio di pantaloni a righe?
Do you have a pair of striped pants?

a quadri
checkered

Preferisci un disegno a quadri?
Do you prefer a checkered pattern?

scuro/a
dark

È un golf grigio scuro.
It is a dark gray cardigan.

chiaro/a
light

Preferirei un colore più chiaro.
I'd prefer a lighter color.

in tinta unita
plain, single color

Preferirei un maglione in tinta unita.
I'd prefer a plain sweater.

colorato/a
colored, colorful

Preferirei un vestito più colorato.
I'd prefer a more colorful dress.

corto/a
short

Questa gonna è troppo corta.
This skirt is too short.

Culture note ⓘ

With leather manufacturing being such an influential part of the Italian fashion industry, Italy is a good place to go for good quality, fashionable leather shoes, belts, and other leather products. There are shoe stores in all

Italian towns and cities with a wide selection of products available.

Florence is known for its specialist leather traditions and prides itself in the quality and style of its products. There are many top leather stores in Florence as well as two very good leather markets. The first can be found in **Loggia del Mercato Nuovo** (the Loggia of the new market), near **Piazza Della Republica**, selling a great selection of bags, belts, purses, and wallets for both men and women. The second is in the area surrounding the **Chiesa di San Lorenzo** (the Church of San Lorenzo) on **Via del Canto de' Nelli**, where you can find similar products.

con le maniche corte
with short sleeves

Ha una camicia con le maniche corte?
Do you have a shortsleeved shirt?

stretto/a
tight, narrow

Questi pantaloni sono troppo stretti.
These pants are too tight.

6

Lesson 1: What are you doing tomorrow?

» How to say "tomorrow," "the day after tomorrow," "yesterday": *domani, dopodomani, ieri*.
» What a reflexive verb is: to wash oneself, to enjoy oneself.
» The present tense of reflexive verbs: *mi lavo, ti lavi, si lava*, etc.
» How to say "going to bed" and "getting up" using reflexive verbs: *addormentarsi* and *alzarsi*.
» The past tense of reflexive verbs: *mi sono lavato/a*.
» How to say you are going to do something: *andare a* + infinitive.

Lesson 2: Booking tickets online

» How to say a train is early, on time, or late: *in anticipo, in orario, in ritardo*.
» How to use the negative with the past tense.
» Expressions using *fare* such as *fare il biglietto, fare il bagno*, etc.
» The months of the year.
» The verb *fare* (to make or to do): present tense, gerund, past participle, and stems.

Collins | Livemocha™

UNIT 6 › LESSON 1

What are you doing tomorrow?

Video Dialog

· ·

Ugo and Lucia discuss their plans for the following day.

 Active Italian: Level 2 > Unit 6 > Lesson 1 > Video dialog

Lucia:	*Allora, che cosa facciamo stasera?*
Ugo:	*Domani ho un appuntamento a Firenze. Devo alzarmi presto per prendere il treno. E tu, che cosa fai domani?*
Lucia:	*Domani mattina, lavoro in negozio. Nel pomeriggio, devo andare ad una sfilata di moda.*
Ugo:	*E domani sera?*
Lucia:	*Vado a dormire presto, perché una sfilata è faticosa!*
Ugo:	*E dopodomani?*
Lucia:	*Dopodomani è mercoledì e ho appuntamento con una cliente in centro.*
Ugo:	*E la sera?*
Lucia:	*Tu mi inviti a cena da Cellini!*
Ugo:	*Ah sì? Non lo sapevo!*

· ·

Lucia:	So, what are we doing tonight?
Ugo:	Tomorrow I have a meeting in Florence. I have to get up early to catch the train. What are you doing tomorrow?
Lucia:	Tomorrow morning I'm working in the shop. In the afternoon, I have to go to a fashion show.

Ugo:	And tomorrow evening?
Lucia:	I'm going to bed early, because a fashion show is tiring!
Ugo:	And the day after tomorrow?
Lucia:	The day after tomorrow is Wednesday and I have a meeting with a client downtown.
Ugo:	And in the evening?
Lucia:	You're taking me out to dinner at Cellini's!
Ugo:	Oh yes? I didn't know that!

Grammar

 Active Italian: Level 2 > Unit 6 > Lesson 1 > Grammar

1 › **Talking about tomorrow, yesterday, and today**

The word for "tomorrow" is *domani* and can be used with different parts of the day.

domani mattina	tomorrow morning
domani pomeriggio	tomorrow afternoon
domani sera	tomorrow evening

The word for "yesterday" is *ieri* and can be used in much the same way.

ieri mattina	yesterday morning
ieri pomeriggio	yesterday afternoon
ieri sera	yesterday evening

The word for "today" is *oggi* and works slightly differently.

stamattina	this morning
oggi pomeriggio	this afternoon
stasera	this evening

Dopodomani is "the day after tomorrow."
L'altro ieri is "the day before yesterday."

2 › ## Reflexive verbs

Reflexive verbs are ones where the person doing the verb is carrying out the action on themselves. For example, washing oneself (*lavarsi*), enjoying oneself (*divertirsi*), or calling oneself (*chiamarsi*).

We use this last verb when we introduce ourselves: *Mi chiamo Max* (My name is Max), *Come ti chiami?* (What is your name?), *Come si chiama?* (What is your name? – using the polite *lei* form).

You will recognize reflexive verbs from the *si* attached to the infinitive: *preoccupar**si*** (to worry), *sentir**si*** (to feel).

3 › | How reflexive verbs work

Reflexive verbs follow the same patterns as other Italian verbs, but include a pronoun (known as a reflexive pronoun) that corresponds to myself, yourself, himself, etc.

Here is the present tense of *lavarsi* (to wash oneself).

mi lavo	I wash myself
ti lavi	you (*familiar*) wash yourself
si lava	he/she/it washes himself/herself/itself
si lava	you (*formal*) wash yourself
ci laviamo	we wash ourselves
vi lavate	you (*plural*) wash yourselves
si lavano	they wash themselves

4 › | Waking up and getting up – both reflexive verbs

Both waking up and getting up are reflexive in Italian.

svegliarsi	to wake up
Mi sveglio alle sei.	I wake up at 6 o'clock.
A che ora ti svegli?	What time do you wake up?

alzarsi	to get up
Luisa si alza alle sette.	Luisa gets up at 7 o'clock.
Quando vi alzate?	When do you get up?

How these verbs differ from other verbs we've seen so far is that they take *essere* as their auxiliary verb (and not *avere*).

5 › **The past tense of reflexive verbs**

Mi sono svegliato alle sei.	I woke up at 6 o'clock.
A che ora ti sei svegliato?	What time did you wake up?
Luisa si è alzata alle sette.	Luisa got up at 7 o'clock.
Quando vi siete alzati?	When did you get up?

Did you notice how the past participles (*svegliato* and *alzato*) agree with the subject of the verbs?
Luisa, being feminine, has a feminine ending: *alza**ta***.
You (*vi*) being plural, has a plural ending: *alzat**i***.

Don't worry; the past participle simply acts like an adjective. Just keep this in mind, though, when talking about yourself, particularly if you are a woman.

6 ›   **The past tense of *divertirsi* (to enjoy oneself)**

This is a chance to remind yourself of *essere* (to be).

mi sono divertito/a	I enjoyed myself
ti sei divertito/a	you (*familiar*) enjoyed yourself
si è divertito/a	he/she/it enjoyed himself/herself/itself
si è divertito/a	you (*formal*) enjoyed yourself
ci siamo divertiti(e)	we enjoyed ourselves
vi siete divertiti(e)	you (*plural*) enjoyed yourselves
si sono divertiti(e)	they enjoyed themselves

7 › A final word on reflexive verbs

Ugo tells Lucia that he has to get up early to catch a train.

> *Devo alzarmi presto per prendere il treno.*

Note how he attaches *-mi* to the infinitive.

If he were telling Lucia to get up early, he would say:

> *Devi alzarti presto.*

If we were suggesting we should get up early, it would be:

> *Dobbiamo alzarci presto.*

It is quite logical, but you must remember to change the reflexive pronoun to match whoever is the subject of the verb.

8 › *Andare a* + infinitive

Ugo tells Lucia that he is going to sleep early that night.

> *Vado a dormire presto.*
> I am going to sleep early.

This is a useful way of saying what your plans are.

Vado a giocare a tennis.	I am going to play tennis.
Vado a fare la spesa.	I am going to do the shopping.
Vado a trovare Max.	I am going to visit Max.

 ## *Vocabulary*

Active Italian: Level 2 > Unit 6 > Lesson 1 > Vocabulary

addormentarsi
to fall asleep

Mi sono addormentato sul divano.
I fell asleep on the sofa.

incontrarsi
to meet (up)

Ci incontreremo domani alle due.
We will meet tomorrow at 2 o'clock.

sposarsi
to get married

Quando ti sposerai?
When will you get married?

cambiarsi
to get changed

Dove posso cambiarmi?
Where can I get changed?

spogliarsi
to get undressed

Non entrare! Mi sto spogliando.
Don't come in! I'm getting undressed.

arrabbiarsi
to get angry

Perché Luisa si è arrabbiata con te?
Why did Luisa get angry with you?

riposarsi
to rest

Sono stanco e vorrei riposarmi un po'.
I am tired, and I'd like to rest a little.

vestirsi
to get dressed

Dovete vestirvi. Partiamo tra venti minuti.
You need to get dressed. We are leaving in 20 minutes.

estivo/a
(in) summer

È una giacca estiva.
It is a summer jacket.

invernale
(in) winter

Mi piacciono gli sport invernali.
I like winter sports.

il paese natale
native land

L'Italia è il mio paese natale.
Italy is my native land.

Culture note ⓘ

When eating out in Italy, there is normally a cover charge, *coperto*, for the table setting, bread, and *grissini* (bread sticks). It is included in the final bill and is charged per person (about 2 euros per person but it can be

more). Service is always included although it is customary to leave a tip (5 per cent is fine). When Italians split the bill they generally share *alla romana* meaning the bill is divided equally.

UNIT 6 › LESSON 2
Booking tickets online

Culture note

You can't buy your ticket on the train. If you don't have a ticket you will be heavily fined. Avoid traveling during peak holiday times – during the week of August 15 (*Ferragosto* – the festival of the Madonna when most Italian businesses and shops close for the week and most cities become deserted for the coast) or Christmas (*Natale*) when there are many foreign and Italian tourists on the move and trains can get hot and crowded.

Video Dialog

Lucia gives Ugo some helpful advice.

Active Italian: Level 2 > Unit 6 > Lesson 2 > Video dialog

Lucia: *A che ora parti domani?*

Ugo: *Non lo so.*

Lucia: *Non hai ancora preso il biglietto?*

Ugo: *No, non ancora.*

Lucia: *Sarebbe meglio prenotarlo in anticipo.*

Ugo: *Perché?*

Lucia: *Perché costa meno.*

Ugo: *Be' adesso è troppo tardi.*

Lucia: *Non è mica vero. Puoi sempre fare il biglietto su internet.*

Ugo: *Ma non so come si fa.*

Lucia: *È facile. Ti faccio vedere io come si fa.*

Ugo: *D'accordo, grazie.*

Lucia: *Figurati.*

....

Lucia: What time are you leaving tomorrow?
Ugo: I don't know.
Lucia: You haven't got your ticket yet?
Ugo: No, not yet.
Lucia: But it's better to book it in advance.
Ugo: Why?

Lucia:	Because it is cheaper.
Ugo:	Well, it's too late now.
Lucia:	That's not true. You can always book your ticket online.
Ugo:	But I don't know how you do it.
Lucia:	It's easy. I'll show you how it's done.
Ugo:	Ok, thanks.
Lucia:	Not at all.

Grammar

• •

Active Italian: Level 2 > Unit 6 > Lesson 2 > Grammar

1 › Early, late, and on time

Lucia says it is better to book train tickets in advance –
in anticipo.

This is also a useful expression when talking about trains, planes,
and buses:

> early is *in anticipo*
>
> late is *in ritardo*
>
> on time is *in orario*.

2 › Using the negative with the past tense

For negatives in the perfect tense, you put *non* before the
auxiliary verb (*avere*):

> ### *Non hai ancora preso il biglietto?*
> You haven't got your ticket yet?

With reflexive verbs, you put *non* before the reflexive pronoun (*mi, ti, si,* etc.):

> ### *Non mi sono lavato.*
> I haven't washed.

3 › **Come? How?**

Questions beginning "How" are introduced by *Come* in Italian. Common questions include:

Come si chiama?	What's your name? (literally "How do you call yourself?")
Come sta?	How are you?
Come funziona?	How does it work?

You also use *Come?* if you haven't heard what someone has said, as in "Pardon?"

4 › **Si – one, you, we, they**

Ugo says *Non so come si fa*. I don't know how it is done. *Si* is an impersonal pronoun like "one".

Si mangia bene in Italia.

One eats well in Italy.

Si sta bene qui.

It is good here (literally "one feels good here").

5 › **_Fare il biglietto_ to buy a ticket**

Fare il biglietto, literally "to make the ticket," is another idiomatic expression using *fare*.

Other expressions include:

fare la spesa	to do the shopping
fare la patente	to study for a driver's license
fare colazione	to have breakfast
fare il letto	to make the bed
fare le pulizie	to do the housework
fare i compiti	to do homework
fare benzina	to fill up with gas
fare il bagno	to go bathing/swimming

6 › *Fare* – an irregular verb

A quick revision of the present tense of *fare* (to make or to do):

faccio	I make
fai	you (*familiar*) make
fa	he/she/it makes
fa	you (*formal*) make
facciamo	we make
fate	you (*plural*) make
fanno	they make

facendo is the gerund (doing, making).

fatto is the past participle (made).

fac- is the stem for the imperfect (was making): *facevo, facevi, faceva*, etc.

far- is the stem for the future tense (will make): *farò, farai, farà*, etc.

7 ›

Months

"Month" is *il mese*. "Monthly" is *mensile*. The days of the month start with a small letter in Italian.

To say the first of a month, use *primo*: *il primo maggio* (May the first). After that, use cardinal numbers: *il due aprile* (April the second), *il sedici settembre* (September the sixteenth).
To say "in" a month, it can be either *in* or *a*: *in giugno* (in June), *a maggio* (in May).

Culture note ⓘ

As with city buses and trams, you need to validate your train ticket before getting on the train. Otherwise the ticket collector can issue you with an on-the-spot penalty. This also applies to the return part of your journey. You must validate your ticket a second time.

Before boarding a train, check whether it is a fast train such as an *Intercity* or *Eurostar* and requires a supplement if you only have a normal ticket (on top of the normal price of the ticket). If you don't, the ticket collector can ask you to pay a surcharge that works out more expensive than the supplement. When buying your ticket you will be charged the correct price if you purchase a ticket for that specific train, but it's always worth checking before you get on board.

Vocabulary

· ·

Active Italian: Level 2 > Unit 6 > Lesson 2 > Vocabulary

gennaio
January

Il primo mese dell'anno è gennaio.
The first month of the year is January.

febbraio
February

Carnevale di solito cade a febbraio.
Carnival usually falls in February.

marzo
March

In marzo il tempo è instabile.
The weather is unsettled in March.

aprile
April

Aprile è il mese del mio compleanno.
April is the month of my birthday.

maggio
May

Le rose fioriscono in maggio.
The roses bloom in May.

giugno
June

Le vacanze estive cominciano a metà di giugno.
The summer vacation begins halfway through June.

luglio
July

A luglio andiamo al mare.
We go to the seaside in July.

agosto
August

Agosto è afoso.
August is muggy.

settembre
September

In settembre si ritorna a scuola.
We go back to school in September.

ottobre
October

In ottobre piove spesso.
In October it often rains.

novembre
November

In novembre comincia a far freddo.
It begins to get cold in November.

dicembre
December

A dicembre ci prepariamo per il Natale.
We get ready for Christmas in December.